Artists' Workshop

Myths
and Legends

Penny King and Clare Roundhill

A & C Black • London

Designed by **Mei Lim**

Illustrations by **Lindy Norton**

Children's pictures by
**Emily Ashworth, Amy Browne, Vanessa Butselaar,
Henrietta Chilton, Amber Civardi, Charlotte Downham,
Purdey Fitzherbert, Tamara Fitzherbert, Claudia Garrod,
James Jarman, Sophie Lewis, Alice Masson Taylor,
Georgie Mew, Victoria Moss, Sam Pepper,
Flora Pethybridge, Susie Roberts, Camilla Schick,
Georgina Smith, Thomas Stofer**

Picture research by **Sara Elliott**

Photographs by **Steve Shott**

First published 1997 by
A & C Black (Publishers) Limited
35 Bedford Row, London WC1R 4JH

Created by
Anne Civardi

Hbk ISBN 0 7136 4744 2; Pbk ISBN 0 7136 4745 0

Printed in Hong Kong by Wing King Tong Co Ltd

Cover photograph: **Antonio del Pollaiuolo** Apollo and Daphne c.1470 - 1480
Antonio del Pollaiuolo and his brother, Piero, worked together for much of their lives.
They ran a very famous workshop in Florence, Italy, where other artists would
come to learn new skills. Antonio was well-known for his interest in drawing
the human body. He was fascinated by the way muscles worked when people
moved and tried to show this in his paintings and sculptures.

Contents

The meaning of myths and legends

In this book, there are six extraordinary stories from around the world. Some are myths, others are legends.

The word 'myth' comes from the Greek word 'muthos' which means story.

These stories usually involve imaginary people and offer explanations to difficult and important questions, such as 'How did the world begin?' and 'Where did people first come from?'

Legends are stories about a real event or person, such as Alexander the Great. Even when he was alive people told stories of his brave deeds.

Over the years, as different people recounted these tales, they added parts to make them sound more exciting and left out the dull parts. Eventually fact became mixed up with fiction.

Many myths and legends from different cultures are remarkably similar. Both Odysseus and Sinbad embark on incredible journeys which last many years, and involve them in fantastic adventures. Stories about a god punishing a sinful world by sending a great flood are found in the Bible as well as in Chinese myths. The more myths and legends you read, the more similarities you will discover.

The six works of art in this book each tell a wonderful story. You will find out how a humble bird helped to create the world and discover the fate of a girl who was chased by an unwanted admirer. You will marvel at Sinbad who faced terrible dangers on his voyages across the sea and meet the hero who saved the world from disaster.

You will see what happened to Alexander when he was lowered into the sea in a glass barrel and learn about King Arthur and his Knights of the Round Table.

Inspired by these magical tales, six artists have used very different techniques to illustrate the stories. Mix their ideas with yours to create your own works of art.

Underwater escapades

Imagine all the wonderful creatures you might see if you were in a glass barrel deep under the ocean! This extraordinary picture comes from a book of medieval tales all about the amazing legendary adventures of Alexander the Great.

During the Middle Ages, books like this one, were very expensive to buy. Only the richest people, often nobles, kings and queens could afford them. Most ordinary people could not read and instead heard tales from travelling minstrels and story-tellers.

The book was exquisitely decorated by skilled craftsmen who used paints made from natural materials, such as carbon, coal, chalk, iron oxides, pure gold and a precious stone called lapis lazuli. The words as well as the pictures were all painted by hand.

Alexander the Great

Alexander the Great was born in 356 BC, in Macedonia, which is now known as Greece. Although he was only 32 years old when he died, Alexander remains a well-known historical figure. He became a famous and victorious soldier, leading his troops across the world and conquering half of Asia. During his life, people wrote of his victories in battle, but in the centuries that followed, these tales became more fantastical than true.

One tale tells of the time, while walking along the seashore, Alexander found an enormous crab clasping some fabulous pearls. After dreaming of more riches from the sea, Alexander made himself a glass-sided barrel, big enough to fit into. Crouched inside the barrel, Alexander was lowered by a long chain beneath his ship until he reached the sea bed. As soon as he found some jewels, he planned to push his hand through a small hole in the barrel, grab the treasure, plug up the hole and return to his ship.

Suddenly, an enormous fish with a mouth as big as a whale's swam up to the barrel. To Alexander's horror, the fish clamped the glass barrel in its gigantic jaws and swam away, dragging the ship behind it. On reaching land, the mighty fish crushed the barrel with its sharp teeth and spat it on to the shore. Although terribly shaken, Alexander recovered but vowed to be much more careful in future.

Secrets of the sea

Create your own magical underwater pictures to go with the story of Alexander inside his glass barrel. Think about the exotic colours, patterns and strange shapes of all the fish, corals and plants he might have seen deep under the sea.

Waxy waters

Use wax crayons to draw Alexander in his glass barrel under the sea with his ship anchored above him. Colour in everything except the sky and the sea. Press hard to make the colours really bright. Wash over the sea with watered-down blue paint. Make the paint a little darker and then wash over the sky.

Underwater scene

Sketch a magical underwater scene with strangely shaped plants, twisting corals, weird sea creatures, exotic fish and perhaps a gleaming palace.

Use your sketch to create a bright and colourful picture. Make the plants and corals from tissue paper and the sea creatures and fish from shiny sweet wrappers. Paint the palace and decorate it with golden glitter.

Tissue paper fish

Draw the shape of a huge fish on coloured paper. Tear lots of fish scale shapes from brightly coloured tissue paper. Stick them on the fish in overlapping rows. Add sequin eyes and frilly fins made from torn tissue or coloured cellophane.

9

Love lessons

This curious picture was painted over 500 years ago
by an Italian artist called Antonio del Pollaiuolo.
He lived in Florence during a new and exciting
time for painters, known as the Renaissance,
which means 'rebirth'.

Antonio del Pollaiuolo *Apollo and Daphne c.1470–1480. Reproduced by courtesy of the Trustees, The National Gallery, London*

Renaissance painters learned how to
suggest distance in their pictures as
well as light and shade. They began to
paint subjects from Roman and Greek
myths, such as this one of Apollo,
the Greek god of sun and Daphne,
a beautiful river-nymph.

Pollaiuolo was also a fine jewellery-
maker, sculptor and drawer. Like many
other Renaissance artists, he had a
large workshop where he trained
young apprentices. Florentine artists
often visited each others' workshops
to share their skills and ideas.

Apollo and Daphne

One day, Apollo came across the god of love, Cupid, clutching his magical bow and arrow. Apollo teased Cupid that his bow and arrow were only toys. To prove Apollo wrong, Cupid took a sharp, gold-tipped arrow and struck him in the heart. Immediately, the sun god fell in love with a beautiful nymph named Daphne.

To make sure that Daphne would never fall in love with Apollo, Cupid swiftly drew his bow once more and pierced her heart with a blunt, lead-tipped shaft. In vain, Apollo begged Daphne to be his love, but the nymph ran away from him, deep into the forest. The faster she raced, the more Apollo fell in love with her.

Daphne ran and ran, her eyes shining brightly and her hair falling about her shoulders like golden clouds. Soon she began to tire. Not able to bear the thought of giving up her freedom, she called to her father, the river god. She pleaded with him to save her by opening up the earth or changing her form entirely. Instantly, her arms began to stiffen and her feet started to twist and root themselves in the earth.

Daphne's soft skin roughened into bark, her arms grew into branches and her hair turned into leaves. Astonished, Apollo reached out to hold her, but instead clasped a slender tree whose leaves trembled at his touch. Cheated of Daphne's love, Apollo vowed to worship the laurel tree she had become, and to always wear a crown made from its shimmering leaves.

The art of love

Make a Cupid card to send to someone you love on Valentine's Day. Or choose your favourite part of the story of Apollo and Daphne to create your own stunning pictures of a river god, a sun god, or Daphne being transformed into a laurel tree.

Valentine card

Make a card out of red, pink or gold paper. Decorate it with bits and pieces, such as ribbon, lacy paper, fur fabric, feathers, paper shapes and sequins. Draw a cupid on black paper and cut it out. Make a bow and arrow out of twisted silver foil and stick them and the cupid on to the card. Send your valentine card with a special message in an envelope decorated with tissue paper hearts.

River god

On pale blue paper, draw a faint pencil outline of a river god with a fishy tail. Paint the top half of his body with PVA glue and sprinkle glitter all over it. Create a strange-looking face from wrapping paper and sequins. Make the god's wild, bushy hair from old Christmas tinsel. Cover his fishy tail with foil scales. Add sequin eyes.

Cut fish shapes out of a flat sponge and use them to print brightly coloured fish all over the background.

Leafy Daphne

Divide a rectangular sheet of paper into three sections. In the first one, draw a picture of Daphne in her beautiful robes with her long, flowing hair. In the second, show her arms beginning to stiffen and her feet starting to twist. In the third, show Daphne transformed into a laurel tree with her rough bark-like skin, her branchy arms and her leafy hair.

Divine dragon

This wriggly dragon, made from ceramic tiles, was created to decorate part of the Nine Dragon Wall in the Forbidden City of Beijing, in China. It shows part of a story about a hero called Yu the Great who was half-dragon and half-human.

Nine Dragon Wall Forbidden City Beijing, China. 18th Century

According to legend, Yu the Great was a brilliant engineer who used his knowledge to save the world from a disastrous flood. For this great achievement he was made Emperor of China. In Chinese art the dragon is often used as a symbol for an emperor.

The Emperor of China was very powerful. Many people believed he was a god in human form. He lived in a magnificent palace within the Forbidden City surrounded by three sets of thick walls. Nobody except him and his servants could enter this secret place.

The legend of Yu the Great

Enraged by the wickedness of the people who lived on earth, the Yellow Emperor, who ruled heaven, decided to punish them by sending a terrible flood.

Only Kun, the Emperor's grandson, took pity on the people. He begged his grandfather to stop the rain, but to no avail. In desperation, he stole some of his grandfather's magic earth and threw it into the floodwaters. Immediately, land began to appear, soaking up the water.

When the Emperor discovered what Kun had done, he had him killed and sent an even worse flood to earth. Day after day, the people were woken by lightning streaking across the sky. Booming thunder echoed through the mountains and huge waves of water crashed against the mountain sides. They picked up their soaking possessions and hauled them to the top of the highest mountain.

Far away, out of Kun's dead body, leapt his son, a mighty dragon called Yu. Yu soared up to heaven and persuaded his great grandfather to stop the flood. Then he returned to earth as a human, only to find even greater destruction. Massive waves crashed over the mountain tops, almost sweeping the last survivors to their watery deaths. It was the work of an evil demon called the Spirit of the Waters who was out to destroy the world. But Yu, helped by an army of spirits, defeated him just in time.

Yu built rivers and dams, lakes and streams to carry the floodwaters away. Gradually, the water subsided. Mountains, hills and fields finally emerged. Now the people had somewhere to live and land to farm. The world was safe.

Heroes and floods

Borrow the beautiful colours and shapes of the dragon in the Nine Dragon Wall picture to create your own One Dragon Wall out of self-hardening clay.

You could also make a magnificent dragon from all kinds of bits and pieces you can find around the house. Or create a stunning flooded landscape picture using thick paint patterned with card combs.

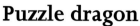

Puzzle dragon

Fold a large square of paper into four squares and open it out again. Draw a simple sketch of a wiggly dragon with bulging eyes, scales and a tongue over all four squares, as shown.

Roll out a large ball of self-hardening clay and form it into a flat square, about 8mm thick. Use more clay to make the shapes of the dragon - his head, eyes, tongue and scales. Look at your sketch to help you. Press the shapes on to the clay tile. You may need to wet the clay to make the shapes stick. While the clay is still wet, cut it into four equal squares, as shown. Leave the clay to harden and then paint the dragon with bright colours. Brush on a layer of PVA glue to make it shine.

Dazzling dragon sculpture

Create your own wiggly dragon sculpture by taping together small cereal packets, cardboard rolls and empty yoghurt pots. Cover them with silver foil and then decorate the dragon's body with feathers, sequins, braid and tinsel as well as colourful pieces of tissue and wrapping paper.

Flooded landscape

Mix paint with flour and PVA glue to make it really thick. Make cardboard combs with different shaped teeth, as shown.

Use a fat brush to paint green hills, dark blue rivers and bright blue sky on some white paper. While the paint is wet, use the combs to scratch patterns in the hills, like those on the Nine Dragon Wall tiles. Make whirly, ripply patterns in the rivers and cloudy patterns in the sky.

Sacred shields

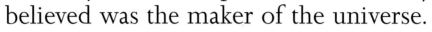

This decorative shield is a copy of one created long ago by the Cheyenne Indians of North America. The picture shows the sacred story of the creation of the earth by the Great Spirit, who the Cheyennes believed was the maker of the universe.

Cheyenne The Earth Diver c. 19th century. The Field Museum, Chicago

Cheyenne Indians led dangerous lives and needed protection from wild animals and from other Indian tribes. A shield, made from buffalo hide, was a brave's most valued possession as he believed it had great spiritual powers.

Shields decorated with pictures of eagles and real eagle feathers were believed to give their owners the power, grace and speed of an eagle. Those painted with bears were thought to provide strength and toughness.

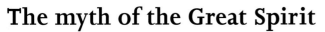

The myth of the Great Spirit

In the beginning, the Great Spirit created the Great Water. There was no sun, no moon and no day, just darkness and the cold, salty sea. Only sea creatures and birds existed. Soon, the birds grew tired of flying around and went in search of land to rest on. The only place where land could possibly be was deep down in the icy water. Again and again, powerful eagles, owls and vultures plunged into the dark sea, but each time they failed to find land.

Eventually, a little coot arrived and, taking a mighty breath, dived into the gloomy waters. Down and down he went, until he spotted a huge lump of earth. Almost out of breath, the bird snatched a tiny speck and returned to the surface.

As he burst through the inky water, the coot saw the Great Spirit glimmering in the darkness. Taking the speck of earth from the bird, the Spirit began to roll it in his hands. The speck began to grow, first into a boulder, then into a mountain, and finally into the whole world. Too heavy for the Spirit to carry, he rested it on Grandmother Turtle's back. Her powerful legs took its colossal weight and the world was safe.

Now, the Great Spirit filled the world with animals, insects and reptiles of all kinds. Lush forests, full of colourful birds, fruits and flowers, began to sprout. Finally, he tossed a burning sun into the sky. Everything bathed in its warm glow as the world started its first day.

Cheyenne creations

Imagine that you need a shield to give you special powers or good luck. Draw a turtle or eagle on it and decorate it with feathers, bells, beads and ribbons. You could also create a glimmering picture of your idea of what the Great Spirit looked like.

Magical shield

Draw a turtle or eagle in the middle of a large white card circle. Decorate it with gummed paper shapes. Use felt-tip pens to draw waves of power coming from the creature's feet. Colour the background with wax crayons, leaving white spaces around the creature and the power lines. Hang feathers, bells, beads, sequins and scraps of fabric from the shield on lengths of coloured wool. Add a loop of ribbon to the top and hang your shield on your bedroom door.

A storm of birds

Fold a sheet of blue paper in half widthways and then open it up again. On the top half, use thick paint and a fat brush to create shapes of birds swooping down to the sea. Before the paint dries, fold the paper again and press the two halves together. Open up the paper and let the paint dry. Use a fine brush to paint in the birds' beaks, feet and eyes.

The Great Spirit

On coloured paper, draw the outline of the shape you think the Great Spirit might be. To make your picture really shimmer, decorate it with tissue paper circles, sequins, glitter, shiny paper and tassels.

Medieval magic

This richly coloured stained and painted glass panel was designed by Edward Burne-Jones and made by William Morris. Both men were leading English 19th-century artists. They created it in the same way as the windows of medieval churches made hundreds of years before.

Edward Burne-Jones and William Morris Arthurian Legends c. 1880-1890 (Detail). By courtesy of the Board of Trustees of the Victoria and Albert Museum, London

The panel shows an episode from the legend of King Arthur. In the picture, Sir Lancelot, one of the Knights of the Round Table is with the king's wife, Queen Guinevere. Although he was Arthur's most trusted knight, Lancelot was deeply in love with Guinevere.

The angel in the red robe is holding a magical golden goblet called the Holy Grail. All the Knights of the Round Table wanted to find this priceless treasure, as they believed it would help them to live forever by healing their battle wounds.

The adventures of King Arthur

When Arthur was a tiny baby, his father, King Uther, told his friend, Merlin, that he feared a plot to kill the child. He asked the wise old magician to keep Arthur safe. When Uther died, only Merlin knew that the king had a son to inherit his crown.

Throughout the land, knights then began to fight each other for the right to become the new king. On hearing this, Merlin asked the Lord Archbishop of Britain to bring the knights to London.

As they gathered in the Abbey churchyard, a massive stone appeared with a sword embedded in it. Only the true king of England would be able to pull it out. Many of the strongest knights tried and failed to pull the sword from the stone.

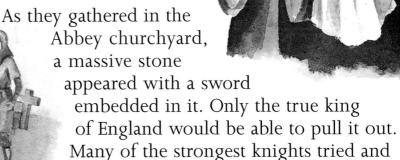

The Archbishop decided to hold a tournament, hoping to find the real king. On his way to compete in it, Arthur's step-brother found he had forgotten his sword. Arthur told him that he would go back and fetch it. As he passed the churchyard, the boy saw the gleaming sword in the stone. He ran up to it and pulled it out without any trouble. At last, the true King of England had been found.

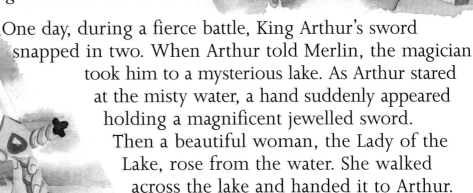

One day, during a fierce battle, King Arthur's sword snapped in two. When Arthur told Merlin, the magician took him to a mysterious lake. As Arthur stared at the misty water, a hand suddenly appeared holding a magnificent jewelled sword. Then a beautiful woman, the Lady of the Lake, rose from the water. She walked across the lake and handed it to Arthur. The new sword was called Excalibur.

23

Stained-glass secrets

To make the stained-glass panel, William Morris cut thin sheets of coloured glass. He attached them to each other using strips of lead - the dark lines you can see in the picture on page 22.

Use glowing colours to create your own pictures from the stories of King Arthur and his Knights.

Glowing jewels

Draw the outline of one of the objects in the story, such as the Holy Grail goblet, the jewelled sword or a crown, on black or gold card. Cut it out. Use a crayon to draw jewel shapes on the back of the card. Carefully cut out the shapes with small scissors. Stick coloured tissue paper over the jewel-shaped holes on the back of the card. Hang your picture on a window where the light will shine through it.

Felt-tip pen window

Choose one of the characters from the stories of King Arthur. Draw him or her on white paper. Place a sheet of thick tracing paper over it and keep it in place with a paper clip. Trace over the character's outline with a black felt-tip pen. Colour in the picture with felt-tips. Frame your picture with black card and hang it on a sunny window.

Stained-glass picture

Lightly sketch a simple scene from one of the stories in pencil on white paper. Over the top of your picture mark out where the 'lead' of the stained-glass window might go. Look at the picture of Lancelot and Guinevere on page 22 to help you. Decorate each section with different colours and patterns using felt-tip pens. Darken the 'lead' lines with a black felt-tip pen.

Arabian adventures

Edward Detmold illustrated this mysterious and exotic scene for a beautiful book called The Arabian Nights. The picture shows part of the story of a dangerous voyage taken by Sinbad the Sailor.

E J Detmold The Voyages of Sinbad from The Arabian Nights. Tales from the Thousand and One Nights 1924. By permission of the British Library, London

Detmold had a twin brother who was also a fine illustrator. From the age of five, the boys made many trips to the London zoo especially to study and sketch animals. Their uncle, who was fascinated by nature, encouraged them to study plants as well.

The painting is not only decorative but also very realistic. Notice the care Detmold has taken to show the rough bark of the trees and the different shaped leaves. The turbans, brightly coloured parrots and flowers stand out from the green of the jungle.

The adventures of Sinbad

Yearning for adventure and riches, Sinbad sailed off on seven perilous voyages around the world. For twenty-seven years he escaped death, survived terrible misfortune, defeated vicious monsters and tricked cunning villains.

On his first voyage, Sinbad and his crew landed on a beautiful island where they lit a fire to cook a fine feast. Suddenly, the whole island began to shake and shudder. Too late, the sailors realized that it was not an island at all, but a huge, angry whale. Luckily, Sinbad escaped to a nearby island. Here, he made friends with the king, Mahrajan, who gave him great riches.

Years later, stranded alone on another island, Sinbad came across a gleaming white palace. As he walked around it, he was surprised to find no windows or doors. All at once, the sky turned black and Sinbad was knocked to the ground by a mighty wind. Hovering above him was a Roc - a bird so huge that it fed its babies on elephants. Only when it settled on the massive white object did Sinbad realize that it was not a palace, but the Roc's massive egg.

On his last voyage, Sinbad was captured by an evil trader who forced him to hunt and kill elephants for their valuable ivory tusks. A wise old bull elephant, anxious to stop the killing, took Sinbad to the elephant graveyard, deep in the forest. Here, Sinbad saw piles of bones and curved tusks. When he told his master about this secret place, the trader was so delighted that he gave Sinbad his freedom, a rich reward and vowed never to kill another elephant.

Voyages in art

Use the stories of Sinbad to create your own magnificent pictures. To help you, look carefully at the leaf shapes of indoor plants and pictures of wild animals. Try to imagine some of the terrifying monsters Sinbad met on his voyages. Perhaps they had razor sharp teeth, huge, curved claws and strange looking bodies?

Fantastic forest

To create a lush jungle scene, cut out lots of tissue paper leaves in different shades of green. Glue them by the stalks only to a dark background. On a separate piece of card, draw one or two parrots. Tear out feather-shaped pieces of coloured tissue paper. Glue them on to the parrot. Stick on a big yellow beak and outline it with a black felt-tip pen. Add some eyes. Carefully cut out the parrot and glue it in the middle of the jungle.

Sunset silhouette

Mix shades of red and orange paint.
Brush wide streaks of each colour on
to a white background with darker
streaks at the top and lighter ones at
the bottom. While the paint is drying,
draw a big egg shape on white paper.
Cut it out and glue it on to the
background, as shown.

Use a white crayon to draw a huge
Roc on black paper. Give it sharp
claws and a curved beak. Cut out
the bird and glue it above the
white egg. Paint on a big
blood-shot eye!

Elephant ride

Use a ballpoint pen to draw an elephant's body
or head on a piece of grey felt. Cut it out
and glue it on to coloured paper. On white
paper, draw a picture of Sinbad to sit on the
elephant. Decorate his clothes and turban
with fabric scraps. Cut him out and glue
him on top of the elephant. Glue on felt
leaves and grass to give a jungly feel.

More about the artists and pictures

Alexander's Submarine
(1445)
The Talbot Master

The Talbot Master was the name given to the illustrator of the picture of Alexander in his glass barrel. The favourite artist of the English Earl of Shrewsbury, John Talbot, he worked in the town of Rouen, in France, and painted 83 illustrations for the stories of Alexander. This book was given, probably as a wedding present, to Queen Margaret of Anjou, on her marriage to Henri VI in 1445.

Apollo and Daphne
(Probably 1470-1480)
Antonio del Pollaiuolo   1432/3 - 1498

Pollaiuolo was an Italian painter, sculptor, engraver and goldsmith. He was famous for his lifelike pictures of people moving their bodies. Pollaiuolo drew his models stretching and bending so that he could see their muscles bulge beneath their skin. He even studied dead bodies, cutting them up to see how the bones and muscles worked in order to make his pictures more realistic. Many other artists did the same, but Pollaiuolo was perhaps the first to be so scientific in his art.

Nine Dragon Wall
(18th Century)
Forbidden City, Beijing, China

The Nine Dragon Wall was a large and expensive project. Many people were involved in its creation. First the court artist drew detailed plans for the Emperor. When the Emperor approved them, they were sent to the province of Shanxi which is famous for its tile making. A team of craftsmen made the tiles out of clay using special tools. The tiles were then painted with coloured glazes and fired in a kiln.

The Earth Diver
Cheyenne Shield   19th Century

A sacred shield could only be made by an experienced shield maker. Together with the bravest fighters of the tribe, he worked in a special lodge. Decorated with bird feathers, the shield-makers sang sacred songs and smoked a special pipe. Before they displayed the finished shield for the villagers to touch, they rubbed white clay all over their bodies. Finally, the shield was placed outside the owner's lodge, where it was turned to face the sun each morning.

Arthurian Legends
(1880-1890)
William Morris   1834-1896
Edward Burne-Jones   1833-1898

William Morris and Edward Burne-Jones met when they were students at Oxford University, in England. They became life-long friends and shared a deep love of medieval tales of chivalry, especially those about King Arthur and his Knights of the Round Table. Together they created many paintings and stained-glass pictures of these tales to decorate the walls and ceilings of churches.

Sinbad the Sailor
(1924)
Edward Julius Detmold   1883-1957

Edward and his twin brother, Charles, worked together on illustrations for storybooks until Charles died suddenly at the age of 24. After his brother's death, Edward began experimenting with different techniques, such as wood-block printing, engraving and still life. However, he continued to illustrate children's books and especially enjoyed painting animals and plants, like those in the Jungle Book, the Arabian Nights and Aesop's Fables.

Other things to do

1 To make a fine treasure chest, paint a small box and lid a bright colour. Brush a thick layer of PVA glue all over the outside and press sequins, paper shapes, beads and glitter into it. When it is dry, cover the box with another layer of PVA to make it shine. Make a fancy key from twisted silver foil and attach it to the box with ribbon.

2 Sketch a picture of what you think a mythical land might look like with all kinds of mythical creatures, strange-looking birds, odd trees and plants as well as exotic flowers and fruits. Colour in your picture with bright felt-tip pens.

3 Create your own mythical monster by drawing a monster face on some bright paper. Glue on scrunched-up silver foil eyes, foil teeth, shiny paper spots and wool hair. Colour the face with felt-tip pens.

4 To make a creation globe, mix flour, water and PVA into a thick paste. Dip newspaper strips into the paste and stick them on to a big blown-up balloon. Overlap six layers of strips, coating the last layer with paste. When the paper is dry, pop the balloon and pull it out.

Paint oceans, ice floes, deserts, forests, mountains and earth on your globe. Cut out card animals, colour them and stick them all over the globe.

Index

Acknowledgements

*The publishers are grateful to the following institutes and individuals
for permission to reproduce the illustrations on the pages mentioned.*
Apollo and Daphne c. 1470-1480, Antonio Pollaiuolo.
Reproduced by courtesy of the Trustees, The National Gallery,
London: cover and 10; The Legendary Journeys of Alexander
the Great by permission of The British Library (Royal MS 15 E
vi, folio 20v): 6; Nine Dragon Wall, Forbidden City, Beijing,
China. Occidor Ltd./Robert Harding Library: 14;
Cheyenne, The Earth Diver c. 19th century. The Field
Museum, Chicago: 18; Arthurian Legends, Edward Burne-
Jones and William Morris. By courtesy of the Board of
Trustees of the Victoria & Albert Museum, London: 22;
The Voyages of Sinbad by permission of The British Library
(12410 t 2) copyright I. MacPhail: 26.